DATE DUE

AMERICAN WAR BIOGRAPHIES

Jefferson Davis

E.J. Carter

Heinemann Library
Chicago, Illinois

Customer Service 888-454-2279
Visit our website at www.heinemannlibrary.com

Designed by Heinemann Library
Page layout by Lisa Buckley
Maps by John Fleck and Heinemann Library
Photo research by Janet Lankford Moran
Printed and bound in China by South China Printing Company Limited

08 07 06 05 04
10 9 8 7 6 5 4 3 2 1

Library of Congress Cataloging-in-Publication Data
Carter, E. J., 1971-
  Jefferson Davis / E.J. Carter.
    p. cm. -- (American war biographies)
  Summary: Profiles Jefferson Davis, who proved himself as a soldier in the Mexican War but had mixed success and failure as president of the Confederate States of America during the Civil War.
  Includes bibliographical references (p.) and index.
  ISBN 1-4034-5082-X (library binding : hardcover) -- ISBN 1-4034-5089-7 (paperback)
  1. Davis, Jefferson, 1808-1889--Juvenile literature. 2. Presidents--Confederate States of America--Biography--Juvenile literature. [1. Davis, Jefferson, 1808-1889. 2. Presidents--Confederate States of America. 3. Confederate States of America.]
I. Title. II. Series.
  E467.1.D26C37 2004
  973.7'13'092--dc22
                                        2003021785

Acknowledgments
The author and publisher are grateful to the following for permission to reproduce photographs:
pp. 5, 7, 11, 15, 19, 22, 23, 24, 33, 37, 39, 40, 41 Library of Congress; pp. 9, 14, 17 The Granger Collection, New York; p. 13 Lise Mitchell Papers/Special Collections/Tulane University Library; pp. 21, 29, 30 Hulton Archive/Getty Images; pp. 35, 43 Bettmann/Corbis; p. 36 Corbis

Cover photograph by Library of Congress

The publisher would like to thank Gary Barr for his help in the preparation of this book.

Every effort has been made to contact copyright holders of any material reproduced in this book. Any omissions will be rectified in subsequent printings if notice is given to the publisher.

Some words are shown in bold, **like this.** You can find out what they mean by looking in the glossary.

Contents

1 Introduction

The nineteenth century was mostly a peaceful period in world history. Few horribly destructive events like the world wars of the twentieth century took place. An exception was the American Civil War (1861–1865), a bitter struggle between northern and southern states over the role of **slavery** and **states' rights** in American society. After the Mexican War of 1846–1848 added new territory to the U.S., debate raged over whether slavery would be extended to those areas, or would remain in the South only. The South grew anxious that the North would eventually try to **abolish** slavery and destroy its way of life. When Abraham Lincoln was elected president in 1860, several states broke away from the **Union** and declared the formation of an independent nation, the **Confederate** States of America. The war that followed was extremely brutal and bloody. After four long years of fighting, the South was defeated and forced back into the Union.

The first and only president of the Confederate States of America was Jefferson Davis. Davis was a cotton grower, politician, and soldier from Mississippi who had led the struggle for states' rights for many years. As a young man he led a carefree and mischievous life as a soldier. But when tragedy struck his family, his personality changed. Davis became a serious and extremely hard-working man. He devoted himself to politics and served as congressman, senator, and secretary of war. History remembers him best as president of the Confederacy.

As president, Davis was faced with the challenging task of fighting a powerful enemy. At the same time he had to build a nation. His government had to write laws, raise money, preserve public order, make treaties with foreign countries, and operate its schools and hospitals. Davis's biggest problem, however, was finding capable generals to fight the Civil War. Robert E. Lee was one great commander he could trust

Jefferson Davis was not very popular with the people of the South during the Civil War. However, after the war he won their respect and affection through his suffering in prison and also through his lifelong defense of the South.

completely. His relationships with his other generals—Albert Sidney Johnston, Braxton Bragg, Pierre Beauregard, Joseph E. Johnston, John Pemberton, and John B. Hood, to name a few—were troubled. He spent much of the war moving generals around, trying to find the right man to lead the Confederate armies in the west. He never succeeded, but both his admirers and his opponents were impressed with the amount of energy he brought to fighting the Civil War.

2   Early Years

Jefferson Davis was the youngest of ten children. His mother, Jane, was 46 years old and his father, Samuel, was more than 50 years old when Davis was born in southwest Kentucky. He was probably born June 3, 1808, although Davis himself was never sure whether he was born in 1807 or 1808. His father struggled to make a living in Kentucky and soon moved the family south to Louisiana, then Mississippi, hoping to become a cotton grower. Eventually they settled on a piece of land near Woodville, Mississippi, not far from the Mississippi River.

Davis remembered his parents as cold and distant, perhaps because they were so much older than he was. He was mainly raised by his older siblings, especially his sisters. He was also close to his oldest brother, Joseph, who would play an important role in his life. Joseph, who was 23 years older, started a law practice in nearby Natchez when Jefferson was still a boy.

In 1816 Davis's father sent him to Kentucky to go to school. He attended a Catholic boys' school for two years before his mother insisted that he return to Mississippi. By then a new school had opened in Woodville, where he studied for five years. He did especially well in Latin and Greek. Many of his teachers were amazed at how well he mastered those languages. When Davis was sixteen, his father again sent him to Kentucky, this time to Transylvania College.

A troublemaker at West Point

While Davis was away, his father died at the age of 68. His brother Joseph, who had become a successful cotton **plantation** owner, suggested that Jefferson attend the

This picture shows Jefferson Davis's boyhood home in Mississippi.

United States Military Academy in **West Point,** New York. Davis was more interested in studying law, but he agreed to try the Academy for one year to please his brother. He wound up staying for four years and graduating in 1827.

Davis was not a very good student at West Point, and he got into a lot of trouble. He was frequently punished for being late or messy, pulling pranks, and drinking alcohol. In 1825 he was caught off campus grounds at a tavern with several other students. The Academy held a **court-martial** to determine whether the students were guilty, and many were expelled. Davis, however, successfully defended himself before the judges and won a pardon. This was his first experience in using his speaking abilities to defend himself.

Davis's behavior was better during his last two years as a **cadet,** but he still graduated in the bottom third of his class. Davis was very independent and rebelled when he felt pressure from authority figures. But he made many good friends at West Point, some of whom would serve as his generals during the Civil War.

Cotton in the South

Cotton was the centerpiece of the southern economy and the main reason **slavery** still existed in the South. The Southern American colonies had been planting cotton since the early 1600s. But when the industrial revolution began in Britain in the late 1700s, European **textile** mills demanded larger supplies. Eli Whitney's cotton gin, invented in 1793, made it easier to separate the cotton fibers from the seeds, and therefore made cotton-growing more profitable. Cotton-picking, however, was still was done by hand, and Southern plantations used slaves to do the work. By the early 1800s, the South was the leading supplier of cotton to Europe's textile industry.

3 On the Frontier

The army assigned Davis to its **Infantry** School near St. Louis. From there he was sent to patrol the frontier in the Michigan Territory. Later he helped take part in the building of Fort Crawford on the Mississippi River, and he also spent five months protecting a group of miners in Dubuque who had fought with nearby Indians. But most of the time Davis was extremely bored. He tried to distract himself with gambling, dancing, fishing, drinking, and horse-racing. Sometimes the officers staged fights between their dogs and wild wolves.

In 1833 Zachary Taylor became the new commander of the First Infantry at Fort Crawford. Davis soon fell in love with his daughter, Sarah Knox, or "Knoxie." Zachary Taylor liked and admired Davis, but he did not want his daughter to marry an army officer. Army men were poorly paid and often sent to distant and dangerous places. When Davis asked for his daughter's hand, Taylor refused. Davis also hurt his chances when he and Zachary Taylor both sat as judges in a **court-martial.** Officers were supposed to wear their full **dress uniforms** when they conducted army business. Some officers voted to make an exception to this rule, including Davis. Taylor, however, voted the other way, and he believed Davis's vote was intended as an insult to him. Taylor and Davis nearly fought a **duel** over the incident.

A second court-martial

Davis himself would soon be on the other side of a court-martial. In April he was assigned to another unit in

8

Lexington, Kentucky. He and Knoxie would be separated. But Zachary Taylor now promised that if the two were still in love after two years of separation, he would not object to their marriage. After gathering **recruits** in Lexington, Davis's new company moved to Jefferson Barracks near St. Louis. Their new commander, Major Henry Dodge, marched the troops during the winter to Fort Gibson, in what is now Oklahoma. Throughout this period Davis, along with the other men, was cold, hungry, and often ill. He began to break military rules. It was only a matter of time before he got into trouble with his officers.

On Christmas Eve 1834, a cold and rainy day, Davis failed to appear for the morning roll call. When his superior officer, Major Richard Mason, demanded an explanation, Davis's response was rude and **insolent.** The major arrested Davis and he was once again court-martialed. During an eight-day trial he struggled to

Zachary Taylor was the 12th president of the United States (1849–1850). He served his country for 40 years as a soldier.

defend himself against Major Mason's charges. Davis refused to apologize and often twisted the facts in his effort to clear his name. He even suggested that it was Major Mason who had been rude and disrespectful. At one point he argued, "Is it part of the character of a soldier to humble himself beneath the **haughty** tone, or **quail** before the angry eye of any man?"

The court-martial made its decision at the conclusion of the trial. Davis was found guilty of failing to appear at roll call and of rudeness to his superior officer, but

Between 1833 and 1835, Davis moved from Fort Crawford, to Lexington, to St. Louis, to Fort Gibson, and finally back to Mississippi.

the court decided that these were not criminal acts. Therefore, he was not guilty of any serious charge. But Davis felt he had been treated poorly, and eleven days later he **resigned** from the army.

Return to Mississippi

One cause of his resignation was his desire to marry Knoxie Taylor. Two years had now passed since Davis left Fort Crawford. Zachary Taylor gave his consent and the two were married on June 17, 1835, in Lexington, Kentucky. Davis brought his wife back home to Mississippi. His brother Joseph had prospered in the cotton business in an area known as Davis Bend, and he gave Jefferson 800 acres (324 hectares) to turn into a **plantation** of his own. The land was covered with tree stumps, shrubs, and prickly weeds. It was such a mess that Davis named it Brierfield. But Davis was determined to turn it into a farm, and he began clearing the land. First he needed workers. His brother loaned him some money, and he bought ten slaves in the nearby city of Natchez. Eventually Davis would own dozens of more slaves.

Southern Mississippi at that time was a wet and marshy place with many mosquitoes. These mosquitoes sometimes carried deadly diseases like **malaria** and **yellow fever,** which they could pass on to humans. That is how tragedy struck Jefferson Davis and his wife only two months after their marriage. They both fell ill from diseases spread by mosquito bites, and on September 15 Knoxie died.

Jefferson Davis lived in this house, named Beauvoir, near Biloxi, Mississippi.

"Old Rough and Ready"

Zachary Taylor was born in Virginia in 1784 and raised on a plantation in Kentucky. He spent his entire adult life as an officer in the U.S. Army, although he also owned a cotton plantation in Mississippi. Known as "Old Rough and Ready," he became famous for leading American troops at the battles of Monterrey and Buena Vista in the Mexican War. The Whig political party decided he would make a good presidential candidate, and he was elected in 1848. His most **controversial** act was to encourage New Mexico and California to apply for statehood without first becoming territories. That way disputes over whether **slavery** would be allowed in those areas could be avoided. Southerners were angry and threatened to **secede.** Taylor in turn declared that he was ready to go to war to save the **Union.** But it did not come to that. Instead Taylor died in 1850 from an intestinal disease.

4 A Career in Politics

Davis almost died from the illness, too, but he eventually recovered. But his spirits were crushed, just when he had escaped the army and was beginning a new and happier life. He went into mourning for many months. He traveled to Cuba for the winter to get better, and the following spring he again began to work on Brierfield. For the next two years he lived with his brother and had little contact with the outside world.

The death of his wife had a deep effect on Davis. His old carefree, playful, troublemaking character was gone. He became a very serious person, devoted to work and study. Joseph Davis had a huge library, and Jefferson spent hours each evening reading literature, philosophy, and history. He gained knowledge of many things that would be useful in his political career.

He also worked hard to improve his land. By 1840 he had 40 slaves working for him, and by 1845 he had 74. Davis adopted his brother's principles in his treatment of slaves. These principles were very unusual for that period. Joseph Davis believed that his slaves would work harder if he treated them well and made them as comfortable and as happy as possible. He gave them as much food as they liked, never beat them, and allowed them to celebrate birthdays and holidays. Most slave owners in the South used brutality, fear, and **deprivation** to keep control of their slaves. Joseph's views on slave-owning were partly inspired by Robert Owen, a British factory owner and writer who believed that workers should control their own environment. Jefferson Davis followed his brother's principles, and he came to believe that slaves enjoyed being

Joseph Davis made his fortune as a planter. He was one of the richest men in Mississippi at the start of the Civil War.

slaves. He never understood that slaves at Davis Bend were treated much differently from those living elsewhere in the South. He also did not recognize how evil **slavery** really was.

As his farm did well and he read many of the books in Joseph's library, Davis grew interested in politics. He met and spoke with political leaders and candidates in his home and began to develop his own views on the important current events of the day. In 1843 he was drafted by the **Democratic Party** to run as a last-minute candidate for the Mississippi State **legislature.** He lost, but he impressed people with his energy and his debating skill.

The following year he ran as an **elector** for the Democratic candidate for president. He toured the state of Mississippi, addressing crowds, developing his speaking abilities, and making himself known to Democrats across the state. Sometimes he was away from home for weeks at a time. The Democrats were successful that year, and James K. Polk was elected president.

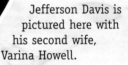

Jefferson Davis is
pictured here with
his second wife,
Varina Howell.

Marriage

In 1844 Davis also met a woman from a nearby **plantation** named Varina
Howell. She was the eighteen-year-old daughter of a fellow cotton grower.
They visited one another frequently that winter, and by March they were
engaged. They would be married the following year. As he struggled to build
a political career, he and Varina also built a house on Brierfield. Over the
years they would have six children together, and Varina would play an
important role in his political career.

Washington, D.C.

Their marriage was sometimes difficult because Davis was so busy and
ambitious. In 1845 he ran for Congress and won. He moved to Washington,
D.C., and tried to make a name for himself. He argued against going to war

with Britain over the territory of Oregon, as some congressional leaders wanted. He helped set up the Smithsonian Institution, the amazing group of museums that preserve American history, art, and culture in Washington, D.C. He also argued frequently for **states' rights,** meaning that the laws and customs adopted by the individuals states should not be interfered with by the federal government. This was a way of defending **slavery** against those who wanted to **abolish** it throughout the United States.

War in Mexico

As Congressman, Davis also argued in favor of the Mexican War. In 1844, Texas, which had been part of Mexico, declared its independence. Later it was **annexed** by the United States. Mexico refused to recognize Texan independence and in April 1846 it sent troops to the Rio Grande. President Polk ordered American forces to confront them, hoping to start a fight, and by May war had broken out.

When the war began, Davis volunteered to lead a group of Mississippians. He was promoted to colonel and led a **regiment** that joined Zachary

The Mexican War lasted from 1846 until 1848. Above is the third day of the Battle of Monterrey, on September 23, 1846.

The electoral college

Instead of directly electing the president, U.S. citizens choose an electoral college. The electoral college is made up of several individuals from each state who pledge to support a certain candidate, as Davis supported Polk. The number of **electors** a state can choose is based on its population. Whichever candidate wins the vote in a particular state sends his or her electors to the electoral college. In a separate vote, usually a month after the general election, the electors officially pick the president.

Taylor's troops just south of the United States–Mexico border. Taylor's job was to prevent the Mexican army from invading Texas, while General Winfield Scott led a second army to attack Mexico City. Taylor's forces met the Mexican soldiers first near Monterrey.

Davis's volunteers were assigned to a spot on the far left **flank.** As they approached the outer fortress of Monterrey, called La Teneria, Davis ordered them to attack. The Mexican defenses crumbled and in an instant the Americans had conquered the fort. Two days later, the entire city surrendered.

Davis further made a name for himself at the Battle of Buena Vista in February 1847. But as he led the Mississippians' charge, he was shot in the right foot. He wrapped his bleeding and shattered limb in a handkerchief, and kept fighting. His men were willing to follow him no matter what after this display of courage. One of them later wrote, "He could infuse courage into the bosom of a coward, and self-respect and pride into the breast of the most abandoned." Taylor's army held its ground during fierce fighting, and the next day the Mexican army retreated.

The injured Davis returned home in 1847 as a war hero. Crowds greeted him at New Orleans when he arrived, and President Polk offered him a position as **brigadier general,** which he refused.

New tensions in the Senate

Davis said no to the position of brigadier general because he had bigger ambitions. His popularity was so great that he was chosen by the Mississippi governor to fill an empty Senate seat. In November 1847 he returned to Washington, D.C. In January he was elected by the Mississippi **legislature** to a full six-year term. The political climate in Washington, however, quickly changed. The war ended with Winfield Scott's conquest of Mexico City on September 14, 1847. With the American victory, the U.S. acquired large territories in the southwest. This brought new life to debates over the extension of **slavery.**

Southerners worried that if slavery was banned from the new territories, eventually the free states would use their large majority to limit slavery or even **abolish** it. Therefore, they fought to allow slavery in the new areas. Davis was a leader of this position in the Senate, and he used his considerable skills to go against attempts to restrict slavery. He began to hint that the Southern states may have to rebel to defend themselves and their customs. He announced that **secession**—breaking away from the United States to form a separate nation—was a possibility for the South.

Robert Owen

Robert Owen owned four **textile** factories in New Lamarck, England. In Owen's time, factories often employed children, some as young as five years old. All workers were forced to work under harsh and dangerous conditions. Owen believed this was wrong. He refused to allow children to work in his factories, and he did not physically punish his employees. He believed that if workers were treated well they would become better people. Eventually society would become perfect. In 1825 Owen founded a **utopian** community in New Harmony, Indiana, based on his ideas.

5 Secretary of War and Secession

In 1852 a **Democrat** named Franklin Pierce was elected president. He made Davis his secretary of war, the **cabinet** position responsible for the armed forces. At first Davis did not want the post, but other politicians convinced him to accept. He was a very active and powerful secretary of war. During the 1850s a number of military **innovations** were developed, and Davis tried to take advantage of them. He hoped to change the American army, getting rid of **corruption** where he could and making use of new technology. One of his strangest ideas was to introduce camels to the American southwest. He believed camels would be more valuable than horses in the deserts of Arizona and California. So he sent a ship to Egypt and Turkey and brought back 54 camels. Unfortunately, the experiment failed. Soldiers preferred horses to camels and the program ended after Davis left office.

As in his other jobs, Davis worked extremely hard as secretary of war. Many people found him pushy and demanding. He was very detail-oriented and insisted on doing things himself. He hated to turn responsibility over to someone else, and sometimes this made him less effective than he could have been. These were characteristics that Davis would display as president of the **Confederacy,** too. Still, he was one of the most important secretaries of war in American history, because he helped the army use the new military technology developing at the time.

Back in the Senate

After Pierce left office in 1857, Davis returned to the Senate. The showdown between North and South was becoming unavoidable. In Kansas the struggle between pro-slavery and antislavery forces was turning bloody. Davis continued to encourage the South to defend itself from **abolitionist** forces in the North. Davis tried to distinguish between "disunionists," who were trying to destroy the United States, and **"secessionists,"** who wanted the right to declare independence if the federal government did not look out for their interests. Many people found it hard to tell the difference between the two groups, and the **aggressive,** sometimes angry, manner in which Davis spoke helped move the nation closer to civil war.

Secession

When Abraham Lincoln was elected president in 1860, many in the South decided it was time to take action. Lincoln belonged to the newly formed **Republican Party.** Republicans did not threaten to abolish **slavery,** but they opposed it being allowed in new states and areas in the U.S. They hoped that slavery would eventually disappear from the country. Some southern states, however, secretly believed that Lincoln and the Republicans intended to destroy slavery entirely. They declared that if Lincoln became president, they would **secede** from the **Union.**

Abraham Lincoln was the 16th president of the United States. He was the first member of the Republican Party to be elected president.

In November Lincoln was elected, partly because the Democrats could not agree on a candidate. Stephen Douglas was supported by northern Democrats, while Southerners voted for John Breckinridge. In December 1860 and January 1861, as southern states seceded one by one, Davis told them to be careful. He wanted to wait to see what would happen after Lincoln took office. Soon, however, the secessionists won across the entire South. On January 7 **delegates** to a special Mississippi convention voted to secede. Davis was in Washington, D.C., during this convention. He also did not attend the meeting in February in Montgomery, Alabama, where a constitution for the Confederate States of America was drawn up. Once the constitution was accepted, the delegates voted to select a president. Each of the states that had seceded so far (South Carolina, Mississippi, Florida, Georgia, Louisiana, and Alabama) received one vote. Davis was **unanimously** elected president of the Confederacy.

6   The New Nation

At first Davis was disappointed. He would have preferred to serve as a general in the **Confederate** army rather than president. He hoped for a short **term** in office. A general election was planned for the fall, and Davis expected that someone else would fill the post then. That spring he had no idea that he would remain president of the Confederacy throughout its four-year history.

On February 18, 1861, Davis was **inaugurated** into office. With his vice president, Alexander Stevens of Georgia, Davis paraded through the streets of Montgomery, Alabama. As he marched to the podium to deliver his speech, a band played the "Marsailles," the French national anthem, since the Confederacy did not have an anthem of its own. Davis then delivered a brief speech in which he wondered whether he had the ability to carry out the job that had been entrusted to him. But he also harshly criticized the North. In his opinion, they were responsible for the collapse of the **Union.**

During the next few weeks, Davis set to work with his usual dedication. His first job was to appoint a **cabinet.** He had six positions to fill, and there were six Confederate states. One representative from each state would be appointed to the cabinet so that all states were treated equally. One of the most difficult parts of Davis's job was making sure states were not angered by the number of government posts it was given.

Once his cabinet had been appointed, he began to build an army and to find generals to lead it. Fortunately, his days at **West Point,** in the U.S. army, and in the Mexican War, made him familiar with many capable military men. He wanted Sidney Johnston, a man he deeply admired, to lead the Confederate forces. He and Johnston fought together in the Mexican War, and Davis knew he was both brave and skillful. Soldiers were devoted to him. Unfortunately, Johnston was in California, and it took time to find him. Other generals, such as Pierre Beauregard and Kirby Smith, wrote to Davis requesting leadership positions. Davis decided that only West Point graduates like himself would be selected as generals.

Davis's other task was to convince the people of the South that the coming struggle was worthwhile. Thus far only a few hundred Southerners had actually voted to **secede** from the Union, and most of them were wealthy **plantation** owners. Davis needed to convince ordinary people that their freedom was under assault by the Union. He tirelessly gave speech after speech, arguing to enthusiastic crowds that the Confederacy had no choice but to go its own way.

Fort Sumter

Meanwhile, Davis had to deal with the first military fight of the war at Fort Sumter. A handful of Union troops still occupied this small fort in South Carolina and the Confederacy demanded that they leave. Davis tried to negotiate with the North, offering payment if the fort were turned over. Lincoln refused to make a deal,

The Civil War began on April 12, 1861, when Confederate forces attacked Fort Sumter, a U.S. army post in the harbor of Charleston, South Carolina.

This is what Richmond, Virginia, looked like during the Civil War.

however, and tried to resupply the fort with food and other necessities.

On April 8, 1861, Davis's **cabinet** met to discuss their options. Davis wanted to bombard the fort if the North refused to give it up. Others, especially Davis's longtime rival, Robert Toombs, argued that the South would be making a bad choice by firing the first shots. No one, Toombs said, would support the **Confederacy** if it started a fight. After a long discussion the Confederate government went ahead with this policy. Pierre Beauregard, who had been selected as commander of South Carolina's defenses, delivered an **ultimatum** to Fort Sumter and its commander, Robert Anderson. When the **Union** soldiers refused to leave, he opened fire on April 12. On the following day, the fort surrendered and the Civil War had begun. Southerners were thrilled at their victory, and admiration for Davis spread throughout the Confederacy.

The Confederacy grows

Davis and many Southerners perceived Lincoln's refusal to hand over Fort Sumter as an act of **aggression.** This act convinced several slaveholding states that had not yet **seceded** (Virginia, Tennessee, Arkansas, and North Carolina) to join the Confederacy. Davis's passionate arguments had won new states to his side. But he was not fully satisfied. Davis believed support for the Southern cause was widespread in states like Kentucky, Maryland, Missouri, and Indiana, too.

Jefferson Davis, seated left center, is shown here with his cabinet. General Lee is standing behind the table, pointing at a document.

The second Battle of Bull Run/Manassas was fought from August 27–30, 1862. The South regained almost all of Virginia as a result of the battle.

He hoped that eventually those states would **secede.** Many of his decisions during the Civil War were made in the hopes of influencing other states to join the **Confederacy.**

When Virginia seceded in May, it invited the Confederate government to use Richmond as its capital. As the home state of George Washington and Thomas Jefferson, Virginia's proposal let the Confederate government claim that it was the "real" America. The Confederate Congress accepted this offer on May 20, 1961, and by May 29 Davis and his family had moved to the new capital.

Meanwhile, Davis continued hiring generals. One of the greatest difficulties Davis faced in picking generals was satisfying all the states. Each state felt that it should have an equal share of the top government and military jobs. So Davis not only had to find the best soldiers, he also had to make sure they came from all the different Confederate states.

Once he had moved to Richmond, Davis, Samuel Cooper, and Robert E. Lee planned the defense of northern Virginia. Cooper was **adjutant** and inspector general and Lee was a close advisor to Davis. Davis believed that the he had to defend every inch of southern territory. But for now the most urgent spot to defend was northern Virginia, which was directly across the Potomac River from Washington, D.C. Already Lincoln had called up thousands of troops to prepare to march into the South. Davis realized the key was to hold the Manassas Gap Railroad. Davis placed Pierre Beauregard near Manassas and Joseph E. Johnston led troops in the nearby Shenandoah Valley. The Confederacy prepared for a **Union** attack.

The first battles

As more northern troops, led by Irwin McDowell, gathered in Washington, D.C., Beauregard and other military advisors urged Davis to take the offensive. But Lee cautioned against this, and Davis agreed with him. The southern troops needed more training before they would be ready to attack.

Instead, the Confederates waited for McDowell to make the first move. On July 21 the two armies clashed. Davis left the capital to watch the battle and found the Confederacy on its way to victory. His army used railroad lines to move Johnston's soldiers in the Shenandoah to join Beauregard at Manassas. Together the two armies were strong enough to fight back the Union advance.

That night Davis met with Beauregard and Johnston and congratulated them on their victory. The three men decided, however, not to pursue the fleeing northern soldiers the next day. Washington, D.C., was too well defended to attack and the South still needed more men and more weapons. This decision would be frequently discussed in the future; some people believed the Confederacy had a chance to win a resounding victory right then and perhaps end the war. But Davis still felt uncomfortable with the idea of invading the North. He wanted to fight a defensive war, showing the world that the North was the **aggressor.**

7   Domestic Problems and Foreign Relations

1861

August
Price and
McCulloch
captured a Union
fort in Missouri

August
Confederate
Congress approved
a $100 million
loan to pay for
the war

November 8
Mason and Slidell
kidnapped on
their way to
Britain

In the months after the Battle of Manassas, Davis's overall strategy fell into place. He decided that the South had to defend three areas at all costs. These were the Potomac River, which divided Virginia from Washington and the **Union;** the mouth of the Mississippi River near New Orleans; and the rest of the Mississippi River. To protect the Mississippi, Davis sent troops to Kentucky and Missouri, states which had not joined the **Confederacy**. He hoped either to build support for **secession** or to take those states by force. An army led by Sterling Price and Ben McCulloch captured a Union fort in Missouri in August 1861, but could not win the state over. Confederate troops also invaded Kentucky, which had declared itself **neutral**. This move probably cost the South some support in that state.

Along with planning military strategy, Davis had other concerns. He basically had to build an entire nation from

This map shows the status of states and territories during the Civil War.

scratch while fighting a war with a much stronger opponent. This was an incredibly difficult task. The Confederacy had to raise money by selling **bonds** to the public to pay for the war. In February the Congress approved a $15 million loan. Later a $50 million loan and a $100 million loan also passed.

Much of this money was paid to foreign countries like Britain and France to buy army supplies. One of Davis's greatest hopes was that these nations, the most powerful in Europe, would recognize the existence of the Confederate States of America. He hoped that would convince the Union to give up the war.

Davis had some good reasons for believing Europeans would support the Confederates. First, they were very dependent on the south for the cotton used in their **textile** mills. If the South refused to sell them cotton, their workers would lose their jobs. But Davis did not realize that Britain and France had large reserves of cotton already, thanks to huge crops in the years before the Civil War. Furthermore, Egyptians were now producing large amounts of cotton and competing with the South. Davis also did not understand that Europeans were deeply opposed to **slavery**. Even if their need for cotton had been greater, many of them would have had difficulty supporting the Confederacy.

Nonetheless, Davis tried very hard to win European support. He argued that the **blockade** the North had set up to cut off southern trade was an act of **aggression** against Europe. He sent a series of **ambassadors** to press his case. Two of them, James Mason and John Slidell, were captured by a Union warship as they traveled in November to Europe on a British ship. Davis hoped this would increase the tension between the Union and the British. But Lincoln quickly handed the **diplomats** over to Britain, ending the crisis.

Davis continued to immerse himself in details, as he had in his previous jobs. Sometimes it seemed like he was trying to do everything himself. He was criticized for not knowing how to trust other people with authority. He also exhausted himself through overwork. Throughout the war he was frequently ill, but he never stopped working.

Slavery

Opposition to slavery grew gradually in Europe during the 18th and 19th centuries. The first step was **abolishing** the slave trade. Great Britain stopped carrying and selling slaves in the New World in 1807 and France in 1818. The U.S. abolished the slave trade in 1808. But even after these laws were passed, slavery continued to exist in colonies controlled by several European nations. Slavery was finally outlawed in British territories in 1834 and in France in 1848. Spain abolished slavery in its territories in 1880.

8 The South Loses Ground

In the west the **Confederate** push to capture Missouri and Kentucky had stalled, and the **Union** was fighting back. In February 1862 Ulysses S. Grant captured two Confederate forts near the Tennessee River. The generals at one of the forts actually ran away from the battle, abandoning their troops. Albert Sidney Johnston, an old friend of Davis's, had returned from California and now commanded the southern defenses in Tennessee. Davis sent the generals Pierre Beauregard and Braxton Bragg to join him, hoping to prevent the Union from marching farther south. He brought in as many **recruits** as possible to help back up Johnston's army. Davis urged the individual states to send him all the soldiers they could spare.

It was not enough. On April 2 Johnston launched a surprise attack against Grant's army at Pittsburg Landing. The assault failed, although it caused heavy damages on the Union. But the day after what became known as the Battle of Shiloh (much of the fighting occurred around Shiloh Church), Davis learned that Sidney Johnston had been killed. Davis wept over the loss of his friend. "The cause could have spared a whole State better than that great soldier," he said. Beauregard took command of the Army of Mississippi.

Fall of New Orleans

Meanwhile, in New Orleans local commanders begged for guns and reinforcements to hold off the U.S. Navy. Davis ignored the pleas. He believed it was unlikely that the Union would conquer the mouth of the Mississippi River without an invading army. But on April 25-26 Admiral David Farragut's **fleet** captured New Orleans and the lower part

Albert Sidney Johnston
was born in Washington,
Kentucky, on February 2, 1803.
He graduated from the United
States Military Academy in 1826.

of the Mississippi. Already the Confederacy had lost one of its three key defensive spots. Embarrassed, Davis replaced Beauregard with Bragg. But no matter how many times Davis changed generals in the west, he never found one he fully trusted and could rely on.

Davis's critics

Criticism of Davis was on the rise during this period. Some Southerners argued that Davis was trying to make too many decisions on his own. He refused, for example, to name a commanding general of the army. The Confederate Congress wanted a general to plan the overall defense of the country, rather than the president. But Davis went against the wishes of the people of Congress on this point, almost to the end of the war. He finally named Robert E. Lee as commanding general in 1864.

The Battle of Seven Pines/Fair Oaks took place from May 31–June 1, 1862. Johnston and the Confederate forces were driven back by McClellan and the Union.

Newspapers could not understand why Davis was not more **aggressive.** They did not realize the weakness of southern forces made that impossible. The early victory at Manassas/Bull Run led many editors to expect a quick triumph for the South. When that did not happen, they accused Davis of making bad choices. Davis and his generals could not explain the true situation because they did not want the North to know how the **Confederacy** lacked men and supplies.

Albert Johnston

Albert Sidney Johnston's early history was very similar to that of Davis. He too was born in Kentucky, in 1803, and attended both Transylvania University and West Point. He served in the U.S. army during the Black Hawk War and later in the Mexican War. Later he moved to Texas and became secretary of war before Texas joined the United States. In the 1850s Johnston served with the Second **Cavalry.** One of his jobs was to escort Mormons to Salt Lake City, Utah. When the Civil War began he made the long journey from San Francisco, where he was stationed, to Texas. After he was killed at Shiloh, he was buried in New Orleans. In 1867 the Texas **Legislature** arranged to have him reburied in Austin.

Davis was criticized for other things, too. To boost the number of Confederate soldiers he created a **draft.** All men between the ages of 18 and 45 were required to serve in the Confederate army for three years. However, some individuals, such as doctors, nurses, government officials, and some wealthy **plantation** owners, did not have to serve in the army. They were considered too valuable to participate in the war effort. Many complained that the poor were forced to fight to defend the right of the rich to own slaves. Finally, when Davis's generals performed poorly, some critics blamed his policy of appointing only **West Point** graduates to top positions. He seemed to be passing up many qualified soldiers.

Union assault in Virginia

Meanwhile, the **Union** general George McClellen was leading his troops on the Virginia Peninsula, to the east of Richmond. Robert E. Lee was now advising Davis on a regular basis. Davis and Joseph E. Johnston, the general defending Richmond, had trouble communicating with each other. Davis's tendency to interfere led Johnston to keep his plans secret, which drove Davis crazy. Davis could not understand why Johnston kept retreating. McClellan moved closer and closer to Richmond, but still Johnston did not attack. Confederate forces were pushed back to the city limits. Davis had to move his family out of Richmond to protect them.

Finally, on May 31, 1862, the battle of Seven Pines/Fair Oaks began. The battle was a **draw,** but Johnston was wounded. Davis picked Lee to replace him. This was the best decision he made during the entire war. Lee was far superior to the other Confederate generals, and he would win many victories in the coming year.

In late June the two armies fought the Seven Days' battle. Lee managed to push McClellan away from Richmond, but could not win a decisive victory. McClellan retreated to the James River, and eventually took his army back to Washington, D.C. Davis and Lee had won some breathing space, and could now think about becoming more aggressive.

9   Reversal of Fortunes

No sooner had McClellan retreated than another **Union** army began marching south, led by John Pope. The Union plan was to bring McClellan's and Pope's troops together into one giant army. But Lee anticipated Pope's moves and defeated him at Manassas before McClellan could arrive. This battle became known as Second Bull Run/Manassas.

On the offensive in Maryland and Kentucky

Lee's tremendous success convinced Davis to trust him. Davis held back his impulse to control the Army of Northern Virginia. Lee was allowed to make military decisions on his own. When Lee decided to invade Maryland, Davis at first wanted to ride up to join the army. But Lee quickly convinced him to stay in Richmond. At the battle of Antietam/Sharpsburg on September 17, 1862, McClellan stopped the forward movement of the **Confederate** troops. They were forced to abandon their invasion of the North. But they had showed that this would not be a quick war. Lee's victories took a lot of pressure off Davis.

Lee was not the only Confederate general on the move in the fall of 1862. Earl Van Dorn and Sterling Price tried to drive Ulysses S. Grant out of northern Mississippi. Kirby Smith was sent to Kentucky to try once again to win that state for the Confederacy. Braxton Bragg followed Smith into Kentucky as well. Over 100,000 Southern troops

Robert E. Lee had great difficulty in deciding whether to stand by his native state in the Confederacy or remain with the Union. Lincoln offered him the field command in the U.S. Army.

were on the move almost at the same time, many of them crossing into northern or **neutral** territory. This was the high point of Confederate success.

But although Davis's generals were holding their own, they were not entirely successful. Van Dorn and Price failed to drive Grant out of Mississippi, and the Union general began to prepare his attack on the key city of Vicksburg. Vicksburg was important to controlling the Mississippi River. In Kentucky, Bragg briefly captured the capital, Frankfort, but soon retreated back to the Cumberland Gap in eastern Tennessee. Bragg was criticized in Southern newspapers for retreating from Kentucky. To try to bring some order to the area, Davis sent Joseph E. Johnston to the west. Johnston had recovered from his wound by now, and Davis wanted him to help improve the **Confederate** performance in that important territory. Joseph Johnston was now responsible for determining the South's strategy in the west.

Davis tours the west

Davis decided to go to Chattanooga to "inspire confidence" in his troops and generals. In contrast to the freedom he granted to Robert E. Lee, Davis tried to control the western area himself as much as he could. In Chattanooga he decided to send Johnston with 9,000 men to Mississippi, where Ulysses Grant was growing more dangerous. This order made Johnston look like he had no power, only a week after he had begun his new job as commander of the west.

Davis continued on to Vicksburg, where he met with John Pemberton, the general defending the city. Davis knew that losing this city would be horrible. It would give the **Union** control of the entire Mississippi River. He wrote to one of his generals, "We can not hope at all points to meet the enemy with a force equal to his own, and must find our security in the concentration and rapid movement of troops." On his way back he gave a speech to the Mississippi state **legislature,** where he tried to make people feel better and defend his own performance: "The wonder is not that we have done little, but that we have done so much." He criticized those in the press who questioned his government and did not tell the whole truth. After a final stop in Mobile, Alabama, Davis was back in Richmond by January 4, 1863.

Emancipation

Much had happened in Davis's absence. The Union Army of the Potomac, now under Ambrose Burnside, again invaded Virginia. Lee had prepared a masterful defense. He easily defeated Burnside at Fredericksburg on December 12. Every general the Union sent into Virginia had been defeated

The Battle of Fredericksburg took place on December 13, 1862 in Virginia. General Robert E. Lee led the Confederacy in a great victory. The Union lost 12,700 soldiers in the battle.

by Lee. But even more significant was the news from Washington, D.C. On January 1, Abraham Lincoln issued the Emancipation Proclamation. The Emancipation Proclamation freed the slaves in the southern states. The war was now more than a fight to preserve the Union. It was a struggle for human rights and racial equality. To Davis, this simply confirmed in his mind that the Union had intended to **abolish slavery** all along.

In Tennessee, Braxton Bragg lost an important battle at Murfreesboro. On January 2 he was forced to retreat 30 miles (40 kilometers) to the south. Davis told Johnston, "My confidence in General Bragg is unshaken." But in reality Davis was worried about Bragg. Many of Bragg's officers were angry at him and questioned his abilities.

10 Scrambling to Save the Confederacy

In May of 1863 Lee won another great victory at Chancellorsville. His army was vastly outnumbered by the **Union's** Joseph Hooker, but Lee sent his best general, Thomas "Stonewall" Jackson, on a secret **flanking** maneuver. Lee caught the Union army by surprise and once again defeated them badly. However, his army suffered a big blow when Jackson was killed.

Gettysburg

As usual Davis was pleased with Lee's performance. But in the west, Grant was moving closer to Vicksburg and something had to be done. Davis and Lee decided another attempt to invade the North might take some of the pressure off John Pemberton, the general defending Vicksburg. In late June, Lee led his army across the Potomac River, through Maryland, and into Pennsylvania. Union General George Meade was sent to confront him near Gettysburg. In a tough battle Lee tried to smash through Meade's lines, but failed. His army was forced to retreat back into **Confederate** territory.

Davis was frustrated that he could not join the fighting either in Pennsylvania or Mississippi. As usual he exhausted himself with his work, trying to get troops and supplies where they were needed. He handled everything himself, even small issues such as the promotion of low-level soldiers. He insisted on reading every single letter he received.

Thomas "Stonewall" Jackson was mortally wounded on October 10, 1862, during friendly fire.

36

Surrender at Vicksburg

One day after the battle of Gettysburg, Pemberton surrendered at Vicksburg. 29,000 troops handed themselves over to Grant's army. The Union now controlled the entire Mississippi River, the nation's most important shipping line. The river divided the Confederacy in half, and made it almost impossible to defend Texas, Arkansas, and western Louisiana. In addition, Davis learned that Union troops had occupied his own land at Davis Bend. They freed his slaves, destroyed some of his property, and stationed soldiers in his home.

The Battle of Gettysburg was a turning point in the war for the North. Casualties in the South numbered between 25,000 and 28,000. Lee would never again have the troop strength to launch a major offensive.

Now the key battleground was in eastern Tennessee. Davis created a new army department and put Braxton Bragg in charge. Bragg won a big victory in September at Chickamauga. But he failed to pursue the retreating enemy, even when urged on by his officers. However, Davis stuck by him, even though by now many of Bragg's men were ready to turn against against him. But once Davis had made up his mind about someone, he rarely changed it. He did not trust certain generals, such as Joseph E. Johnston and Beauregard, no matter what they did. But with others, like Bragg and Sidney Johnston, he remained loyal even when they made big mistakes. This, for better or worse, was one of Davis's main characteristics.

Slaves as soldiers?

Meanwhile, the situation for ordinary people in the South was becoming desperate. **Riots** broke out in the streets because there was no food. Davis did what he could to keep order. Southerners also were furious when the Union began using all-black **regiments.** Davis declared that any captured black soldier would be returned to **slavery.** But the lack of manpower in the Confederate army raised questions over whether the South should use slaves in its own army. Some Southerners wondered whether they would have to give rights to blacks in order to survive as a nation. Davis rejected the idea, but later he would change his mind.

11 The Rebellion Crumbles

Davis's faith in Bragg did not pay off. On November 25, 1863, Bragg was **routed** by Grant at Chattanooga, and **resigned** his post. His officers, and much of the nation, had completely lost confidence in him. Davis immediately asked Lee to leave Virginia and take command in Tennessee. Lee refused, saying he did not know the men or the land in Tennessee. Davis felt he had to accept Lee's refusal. The Virginian was too famous and beloved by Southerners to order him to do something he did not want to do. Instead, Davis asked Joseph E. Johnston to replace Bragg.

Johnston retreated from William T. Sherman's army, just as he had retreated from McClellan early on in the war. Davis grew frustrated, even though Sherman had a much bigger army. Johnston was trying to preserve his troops as long as possible, but Davis wanted a showdown. He even thought of traveling to Atlanta to take command himself. But on July 18, 1864, he decided to replace Johnston with John B. Hood. Hood was young and inexperienced, but bold and ambitious. Under the circumstances, these qualities did not work well together. In a daring move, Hood attacked William T. Sherman's forces near Atlanta four times. He was unsuccessful. Instead of a long **siege** of Atlanta, Sherman quickly overran the city. Sherman then began what would become known as his march to the sea. Destroying everything in his path, he tried to convince Southerners to stop fighting.

Congress investigates Davis

As Davis watched his armies fall apart, his political reputation was in trouble. The **Confederate** Congress attacked Davis and called for an investigation of the battles of Vicksburg and Chattanooga. Many Congressmen believed these losses were caused by mistakes made by Davis. Some Southerners argued that the Confederate government was proving to be better than the **Union** government. They used the **states' rights** argument to challenge Davis's authority. As Sherman's troops marched through Georgia, rumors spread that Georgia might rejoin the United States.

Grant's push against Lee

Meanwhile, Ulysses S. Grant had become general-in-chief of the **Union** army. He focused on defeating Lee's Army of Northern Virginia. After a month of bloody fighting, Grant laid siege to Petersburg, an important town south of Richmond. For months the armies rarely fought. Each side was waiting to learn the outcome of the 1864 U.S. presidential election. If Lincoln lost, the South might be able to make a deal with the new Union leader without suffering total military defeat. In November Lincoln was re-elected, however, and the war went on.

The following spring, Grant mounted a major offensive. His army broke through Lee's lines and the Confederates fled in retreat. When Petersburg fell on April 2, thousands of people fled from nearby Richmond, including Davis and his family. He relocated to Danville, near the North Carolina border. For a few days this became the new capital of the **Confederacy.**

In 1864, Joseph E. Johnston was relieved of duty by Jefferson Davis, who believed Johnston was too afraid to fight. Johnston did not command again until 1865.

Braxton Bragg

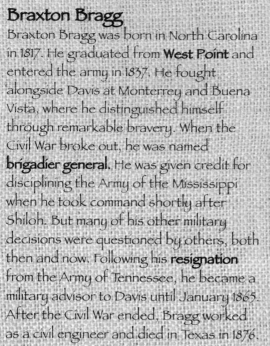

Braxton Bragg was born in North Carolina in 1817. He graduated from **West Point** and entered the army in 1837. He fought alongside Davis at Monterrey and Buena Vista, where he distinguished himself through remarkable bravery. When the Civil War broke out, he was named **brigadier general.** He was given credit for disciplining the Army of the Mississippi when he took command shortly after Shiloh. But many of his other military decisions were questioned by others, both then and now. Following his **resignation** from the Army of Tennessee, he became a military advisor to Davis until January 1865. After the Civil War ended, Bragg worked as a civil engineer and died in Texas in 1876.

Davis's last stand

But the war was nearly over. Lee was having trouble supplying his troops, and he surrendered to Grant on April 9 at Appomattox Court House. But Davis refused to give up. He told his associates that if necessary he would take to the hills and continue to fight the North. He moved again to Greensboro, North Carolina. He met with Joseph E. Johnston, whose army had not yet surrendered. On April 11, 1865 Johnston, along with Beauregard declared that it would be best to give up. "It would be the greatest of human crimes for us to attempt to continue the war," Johnston argued. The majority of Davis's **cabinet** also voted to surrender Johnston's army to Sherman. But Davis himself wanted to keep fighting. "We can whip the enemy yet, if our people will turn out."

Varina urged him to keep fighting as well. She suggested they travel to Texas, where they might still have supporters. With a small party they continued to make their way slowly across Georgia. But on the night of May 9, **Union** soldiers caught up with them outside the town of Abbeville. As Davis attempted to sneak away, he grabbed his wife's shawl to hide himself. He was quickly caught by the soldiers. Soon the story spread that Jefferson Davis was dressed in women's clothing when he was arrested. Northerners would ridicule him for many years for being caught in this manner. By humiliating Davis they hoped to convince Southerners to give up their resistance for good.

This cartoon was created shortly after Davis's capture by Union troops. Davis, dressed as a women in center, holds a bucket with the initials "C.S.A." The initials stand for **Confederate** States of America. "Old Mother" is underlined to emphasize that Davis is dressed as a woman. His deceit was viewed as very cowardly.

I see that old Mother wears Whiskers too.

If you hadn't taken us Women & Children by surprise we wouldn't have surrendered without a fight.

It strikes me your old Mother wears very big Boots.

Please let my old Mother go to the Spring for some Water to wash in.

A "SO CALLED PRESIDENT" IN PETTICOATS.

12 Life After War

Davis was taken to Fort Monroe, a military camp off the coast of Virginia. In May a federal court charged him with **treason.** He was held for two years. This, too, was part of a strategy to discredit Davis in Southern eyes. At one point he was even placed in leg irons. This, however, went too far. Even Northerners protested against this cruel treatment, and after five days the irons were removed.

Davis hoped a trial would take place. He believed he could convince the public that he was right, just as he had defended himself in **court-martials** as a young man. Finally, on May 11, 1867, he was released from prison on $100,000 bail. Davis went to Montreal, Canada, where his family had been living since the war ended. But he never got his trial. It was repeatedly delayed until December 5, when all charges were dropped.

Insurance company executive

Davis lived many years after the war ended. His main concerns were to make money and to save his reputation. At first his family was desperate for money. His legal fees had been expensive, and his family had no source of income while he was in prison. Brierfield had been seized by the U.S. government after the war and given to former slaves. Davis went to court to try to get it back, but it was not returned to him until 1881.

Davis took a job as president of the Carolina Life Insurance Company, which was located in Memphis, Tennessee. He held that position until 1873. Later he worked for the Mississippi Valley Association, which promoted trade between European nations and the South. He and his family spent much time in England.

Memoirs

In 1876 Davis began writing his war **memoirs.** He tried to defend himself against Northerners who believed he had committed treason in **seceding** from the **Union.** But he also had to reply to those Southerners who believed he was a poor leader. He finally finished the memoirs in 1881. He was very disappointed, however, in the slow sales of the book. He wrote two other books, a history of the **Confederacy** and an autobiography, but neither was successful.

On December 6, 1889, Jefferson Davis died at the age of 81 or 82. By that time the bitter feelings of the past had begun to fade. An incredible 200,000 people attended his funeral, probably the biggest funeral ever in the South. The mourners remembered Davis as someone who fought passionately and persistently for what he believed in. Although he made mistakes as president, he faced an extremely difficult task. The Union was simply too large and too powerful to be defeated, no matter who was president of the Confederacy.

Davis was one of the most important politicians in American history. For almost twenty years, he was the leading spokesman for **states' rights** in the South. When the Confederate states seceded, he was a natural choice to be president. Although some Southerners were not pleased with Davis's leadership during the war, no one else with better ideas and broader popularity ever surfaced. He never enjoyed the heroic status among Southerners that Robert E. Lee achieved, but the mark he left on history was deeper.

Davis published *The Rise and Fall of the Confederate Government* in 1881. The book was meant to defend himself and his actions to his critics.

Timeline

June 3, 1807 or 1808	Jefferson Davis born in Kentucky
1810 or 1811	Davis family moved to Mississippi
1816	Davis sent to school in Kentucky
1818	New school opened in Woodville, Mississippi
Spring 1823	Davis sent to Transylvania College
1824–1827	Davis attended the U.S. Military Academy
1825	Davis **court-martialed** for breaking campus rules
January 1829	Davis reported for duty at Jefferson Barracks in St. Louis
March 1829	Davis assigned to duty in the Michigan Territory
January 1833	Met Sarah "Knoxie" Taylor
February 12, 1835	Court-martial for insulting an officer began
June 17, 1835	Davis married Knoxie Taylor
August 1835	Davis purchased his first slaves
September 15, 1835	Knoxie died, probably from **yellow fever** or **malaria**
Fall 1843	Davis lost race for Mississippi State **Legislature**
January 1844	Met Varina Howell
Fall 1844	Ran as **elector** for James K. Polk
March 1845	Davis married Varina Howell
November 1845	Elected to Congress; moved to Washington, D.C.
1846–1847	Led Mississippi volunteers in the Mexican War
January 1848	Elected to U.S. Senate
Spring 1852	Davis named secretary of war
Spring 1857	Returned to the Senate
November 1860	Abraham Lincoln elected president of the United States
December 20, 1860	South Carolina became the first state to **secede** from the **Union**
January 7, 1861	Mississippi voted to secede
January 21, 1861	Davis **resigned** from the Senate
February 9, 1861	Davis **unanimously** elected president of the **Confederacy**
February 18, 1861	Davis **inaugurated** as president
April 12, 1861	First shots at Fort Sumter; start of Civil War
May 29, 1861	Confederate capital moved to Richmond, Virginia
June 8, 1861	Tennessee became the eleventh and last state to join the Confederacy
July 21, 1861	Battle of Manassas/Bull Run; first major battle of the war
August 1861	Price and McCulloch captured a Union fort in Missouri; Confederate Congress approved a $100 million loan to pay for war
November 8, 1861	Mason and Slidell kidnapped on their way to Britain

February 1862	Ulysses S. Grant captured two Confederate forts in Tennessee
April 2, 1862	Battle of Pittsburg Landing/Shiloh; Sidney Johnston killed
April 25–26, 1862	Admiral Farragut captured New Orleans for the Union
May 31, 1862	Battle of Seven Pines/Fair Oaks; Joseph E. Johnston wounded and Robert E. Lee took command of the Army of Northern Virginia
April 16, 1862	**Draft** law passed in Confederate Congress
August 28–30, 1862	Second battle of Manassas/Bull Run
September 17, 1862	Battle of Antietam
December 10, 1862	Davis toured the West, visiting troops at Chattanooga and Vicksburg
December 13, 1862	Battle of Fredericksburg
December 31, 1862	Battle of Murfreesboro
January 1, 1863	Emancipation Proclamation
May 12, 1863	Battle of Chancellorsville
July 1–3, 1863	Battle of Gettysburg
July 4, 1863	Fall of Vicksburg to Grant
July 18, 1863	First use of all-black **regiments** by Union
July 25, 1863	Bragg named command in Tennessee
July 1863	Union troops take Davis Bend
November 25, 1863	Battle of Chattanooga
December 7, 1863	Confederate Congress began investigation of Vicksburg and Chattanooga
December 8, 1863	Davis asked Lee to take command in Tennessee
May–June 1864	Wilderness, Spotsylvania, Mule Shoe, Cold Harbor, and Petersburg campaigns
July 18, 1864	Johnston replaced with Hood
May 11, 1867	Davis released from prison
December 5, 1867	**Treason** charge against Davis dropped
1881	Davis published **memoirs**
December 6, 1889	Davis died

Further Reading

Brewer, Paul. *The American Civil War.* Chicago: Raintree, 1999.

Isaacs, Sally Senzell. *America in the Time of Abraham Lincoln (1815–1869).* Chicago: Heinemann Library, 1999.

Naden, Corinne J., and Rose Blue. *Why Fight? The Causes of the American Civil War.* Chicago: Raintree, 2000.

Smolinski, Diane. *Key Battles of the Civil War.* Chicago: Heinemann Library, 2001.

Smolinski, Diane. *Soldiers of the Civil War.* Chicago: Heinemann Library, 2001.

Glossary

abolish officially put an end to something; an abolitionist was a person who demanded that slavery be ended in the South

adjutant staff officer in the military who assists a commanding officer

aggression fierce or threatening behavior

ambassador person from one country sent on a government mission to another country

annex take control of another country by force

blockade using warships to cut off trade between a territory and the outside world

bonds papers a government sells to raise money

brigadier general military officer who is one rank above a colonel

cabinet president's main advisors

cadet student in a military academy

cavalry soldiers who ride horses

Confederacy eleven Southern states that seceded from the United States between 1860 and 1861; a Confederate is a supporter, citizen, or soldier of the Confederacy

controversial causing or related to controversy, a long or heated discussion about something that people have a great difference of opinion about

corruption behaving in a bad or improper way; to change from good to bad

court-martial military trial

delegate person sent as a representative to a meeting or conference

Democratic Party political organization formed by people who believed that government should be elected by the nation's people

diplomat person who represents his or her country's government in a foreign country

draft method of selecting people to serve in the army

draw both sides of a competition are even

dress uniform soldier's uniform worn for formal events

duel battle fought with weapons between two persons; duels have formal rules and require witnesses

elector member of a group that chooses the president of the United States; the electors are chosen by the vote of the people

flank far right or left end of an army's line of troops

fleet group of warships under one command

haughty description for a person who is very proud and looks down on other people

inaugurate swear a public official into office with a formal ceremony; the day an official is sworn in is known as the inauguration day

infantry soldiers who walk, the main part of an army

innovation new idea or invention

insolent insulting and outspoken

legislature group of people who have the power to make or change laws for a country or state

malaria tropical disease that people get from a virus carried by mosquitoes

memoir story of a person's experiences and life

neutral not favoring either side in a fight, contest, or war

plantation large farm on which crops are tended by laborers who also live there

quail lose courage or shrink in fear

recruit find new members; one of those new members is called a recruit

regiment military unit

Republican Party political organization formed by people opposed to slavery who felt that the United States government should not allow and abolish slavery in its new territories

resign quit or give up a job or other responsibility

riot group of people that behave in a noisy, violent, and usually uncontrollable way

rout beat badly

secede separate from a larger unit, such as the Union; a person who supports seceding is called a secessionist

siege long assault on a town or fortress

slavery owning other human beings and forcing them to work

states' rights view that the laws and customs adopted by the individuals states, including slavery, should not be interfered with by the federal government.

term definite or limited period of time

textile clothes or cloth

treason act of betrayal, such as against a country or government

ultimatum demand that if refused will bring about an end to peaceful talks and that could lead to actions of force

unanimously agreed on by everyone

Union another name for the United States of America; during the Civil War it referred to the states that remained loyal to the United States government

utopian ideal and perfect, especially in terms of government, social conditions, and laws

West Point United States Military Academy at West Point, New York. Lee and most of the major Civil War generals attended it.

yellow fever infectious tropical disease marked by yellow skin and vomiting that people get from a virus carried by mosquitoes

Index